THE SUPREME COURT

THE
SUPREME
COURT

BY HAROLD COY
Revised By
LORNA GREENBERG

A First Book/Revised Edition
Franklin Watts
New York/London/Toronto/Sydney/1981

Photographs courtesy of:

Monkmeyer Press Photo Service (Feily):
frontispiece;
United States Supreme Court:
p. 5;
United Press International:
pp. 15, 44;
Wide World Photos:
pp. 19, 27, 35;
New York Public Library Picture Collection:
p. 29;
The Supreme Court Historical Society:
p. 47.

Library of Congress Cataloging in Publication Data

Coy, Harold.
The Supreme Court.

(A First book)
Originally published in 1958 under title:
The First book of the Supreme Court.
Includes index.
SUMMARY: Explains the structure and functions
of the Supreme Court, how cases come before it,
and the various legal rights of a citizen.
1. United States. Supreme Court—Juvenile literature.
[1. United States. Supreme Court]
I. Greenberg, Lorna. II. Title.
KF8742.Z9C6   1981   347.73′26   80–25701
ISBN 0–531–04252–9

CONTENTS

THE SUPREME COURT

HOW WOULD YOU DECIDE THIS CASE?

Mrs. Julia V. Miller adored the red cedars at her country home in Virginia. The saplings made nice Christmas trees. When the bigger trees were thinned out, she sold the logs for fence posts. Best of all, the grove was ornamental. It added beauty to her home.

The apple growers of the neighborhood did not share Mrs. Miller's enthusiasm for red cedars. Every spring breeze carried the spores of the cedar rust disease from her grove into their orchards.

Cedar rust is an odd plant disease. It rocks along quietly in the cedar boughs, seemingly content to live and let live. Once it gets among apples, though, it cuts loose, sparing neither leaves nor fruit. But it can't keep going without that quiet period on the cedars.

The apple growers grew more and more unhappy watching their fine Albemarle pippins turn rust-spotted and knobby. They showered complaints on State Entomologist W. J. Schoene. After investigating, he told Mrs. Miller it was too bad, but she would have to cut down the cedar grove.

"It's the law," he explained, going on to tell her about Virginia's Cedar Rust Act for the protection of apple growers. Cut down the cedars, and the rust goes too.

Mrs. Miller protested, "I am a cedar grower. I have as much right to my property as the apple growers have to theirs." Her mind made up, she hired a lawyer and fought for her cedars all through the state courts. She lost. But there was still a chance. Her lawyer went to the highest court in the land, the Supreme Court of the United States. Her case was known as *Miller* v. *Schoene* (Miller *versus*, or against, Schoene). Cases before the Supreme Court are called by titles made up of the names of the parties involved—the loser of the case in the lower court against the winner.

Mrs. Miller's lawyer claimed that the Virginia law was contrary to the Constitution of the United States. It took away one person's property to help another person. The value of Mrs. Miller's property would shrink without her beautiful trees! Apple growers had no right to shift their misfortunes to cedar growers, Mrs. Miller's lawyer said.

Mr. Schoene's lawyer praised Virginia's famous apples. Orchards worth millions of dollars would die if cedars remained. Thousands of jobs would melt away. No one had a right to injure the state's prosperity, he claimed.

How would you decide this case? Would you tell Mrs. Miller to cut down her trees, or would you tell Mr. Schoene to leave them alone?

Here's what the Supreme Court decided. Something had to go, apples or cedars; the state had to make a choice. In such circumstances, said the Court, the state had the power to decide upon the destruction of one class of property in order to save another which, in the judgment of the legislature, was of greater value to the public.

That was the end of Mrs. Miller's cedars. The law was on the side of Mr. Schoene and the apples.

"IT'S THE LAW OF THE LAND"

The case of the cedars versus the apples brings out the following points: A state may pass reasonable laws to protect the safety and health of its people. But a state law which conflicts with the United States Constitution must give way. The Constitution, for example, safeguards a person's property rights. At the same time, the neighbors have a right to be safe from harm. One right must sometimes be balanced against another.

The Supreme Court has to decide these matters. It holds the delicate balance between freedom and authority . . . between private property and public welfare . . . between the states and the nation. When the Supreme Court speaks, it has the final say as to what the law is. The Court can be overruled only by the people of the United States, who may vote to amend the Constitution, the law of the land.

WHAT IS THE SUPREME COURT?

The Supreme Court—and the Constitution by which it was created—are American inventions. When the founders of the United States gathered in Philadelphia in 1787, they set out to develop an improved plan for the government of their young country. They were still smarting from the wrongs done them by the British king's officials before the Revolution, and had very clear ideas of what they didn't want their government to become. The document they produced—the Constitution of the United States—set the outlines for a national government that would be strong enough to hold the country together and protect the lives and property of the people; but that would also foster and safeguard the people's rights and individual freedoms. The Bill of Rights—the first ten amendments to the Constitution, adopted in 1791—provides specific guarantees of these rights.

The founders divided the powers of the government among

[3]

three parts, or branches: the legislative branch, the executive, and the judicial. The **legislative** branch, Congress, was given the right to make laws (pass legislation). The **executive** branch, under the President, the chief executive, was given the power to put the laws into effect. The **judicial** branch, or judiciary, was entrusted with judicial power—the power to decide cases under the laws. The judiciary was to consist of one Supreme Court and such lower courts that Congress would deem necessary to establish.

Besides dividing the functions of government between three separate branches, the framers of the Constitution were also careful to set up a **government of limited powers.** Some powers were given to the federal government; others were reserved for the states. The Constitution lists things Congress, the President, and the Court have the right to do. Besides these "cans," it also lists "can'ts"—things the federal government can't do, things the states can't do, and some that may not be done by any government.

The "cans" and "can'ts" of the Constitution are not like other ordinary laws that can be wiped away by a simple vote of representatives. Changing the Constitution is a hard, slow process. It was planned that way so that changes—constitutional amendments—would require plenty of debate and thought.

The Constitution forbids Congress or state legislatures from passing two specific kinds of laws. Neither can pass a law saying, "Joseph Doakes is a rascal and shall be hanged." This law would be a **bill of attainder**—it finds Joseph guilty without a trial. They cannot pass a law saying, "What Joseph Doakes did yesterday is a crime." This would be an **ex post facto law** (from Latin words meaning, "from a thing done afterward"). It would punish a person for something that was not a crime when the person did it.

[4]

*The Seal of the Supreme Court, ordered by
the Justices in 1790 at their third meeting.
The designers adapted the Great Seal of the United States,
adding a single star below the American eagle
to symbolize the Constitution's grant of
judicial power to "one Supreme Court."*

Suppose such a law is passed anyway, and Joseph is arrested and brought to trial. The judge studies the new law, then looks into the Constitution and reads that no such law may be passed. The judge must choose between the two laws: the new one and the Constitution. The judge must rule that the Constitution is the higher law, and that therefore the new law is **unconstitutional** and of no effect. If the judge doesn't rule this way, Joseph's lawyer will surely **appeal** the case (take it for review) to a higher court.

Article VI of the Constitution says that **the supreme law of the land** is "The Constitution, Laws of the United States made under it, and Treaties made under the authority of the United States."

If a federal law conflicts with the Constitution (as the bill of attainder against Joseph does), that law is unconstitutional, for the Constitution is the highest law. Laws and treaties that Congress has the right to make are supreme over conflicting state laws. And judges in state courts must give right of way to the supreme law of the land.

The Supreme Court can decide whether federal or state laws, or an executive action, conflict with the Constitution. Although this power— called **judicial review**—was not specifically given to the Court in the Constitution, many of its framers expected the Court to take on this responsibility. One of the Court's most important early decisions established the power of judicial review. In *Marbury* v. *Madison* (1803), the Court ruled that it had a duty to guard the Constitution. If a law passed by Congress or a state legislature was in conflict with the Constitution, the Court had to decide in favor of the Constitution. Chief Justice Marshall said it was the "province and duty of the judicial department, to say what the law is."

Since that ruling, the Court's right to exercise the power of judicial review has been firmly established. This power—which allows the Court to strike down a law passed by Congress or a state, or stop an action of the President—has made the Court a strong force.

In the case of Joseph Doakes, it is easy to see how the law conflicts with the Constitution. But most cases are not that clear. Many court decisions, no matter which way they go, are appealed—the losing side takes the case to a higher court for review. A few cases work their way up through the court system to the Supreme Court. That court has the final word.

HOW CASES REACH THE COURT

"I'll win this case if I have to take it all the way to the Supreme Court!"

That's what many people say on starting a lawsuit. But very few cases get that far.

The Supreme Court is the final authority on the law of the land. Below it are two independent networks of courts that operate alongside each other: a state court network and a federal one. To reach the Supreme Court, cases usually have to work their way up through one of these networks.

State courts are the arenas for most criminal cases and most disputes between people. A suit begins in a local trial court. If the losing party believes the verdict was wrong, or unfair, or that there was a mistake in the trial, the case can be appealed to a state **appellate court.**

From the highest state appellate court to the Supreme Court is a big step, and a case can be carried there only if a substantial **federal question** is involved. A "federal question" means a question on the meaning of the Constitution, or a federal law or treaty. One example would be if a person claimed that a state court had denied that person's federal constitutional rights.

Federal courts try cases involving federal laws—about patents, bankruptcy, or naturalization, or crimes such as mail theft or counterfeiting. The lowest courts in the federal network are **United States District Courts.** If a case is appealed, it is heard in a **United States Court of Appeals.** This is usually the last stop for federal cases. Certain types of appeals that involve the constitutionality of federal laws may go from District Court directly to the Supreme Court, leapfrogging over the Court of Appeals.

Congress has also created special federal courts—Tax Court, Customs Court, Court of Customs and Patent Appeals, Court of Claims (which hears claims against the federal government). Appeals from the Court of Claims are heard directly by the Supreme Court. The Customs Court sends appeals first to the Court of Customs and Patent Appeals; and then to the Supreme Court; Tax Court appeals are heard first in a United States Court of Appeals.

From its position above all the courts of the land, the Supreme Court has the jurisdiction to review cases from federal courts, cases from state courts if they concern a federal question, and cases from special courts. But the Court could not possibly hear all the cases that parties would like to bring before it. The Justices sift the cases and select those which, as Justice Potter Stewart has said, "raise the most important and far-reaching questions."

Every year the Court is faced by about 4,500 cases. There are a few types that Congress has said the Court must review, and these are brought to the Court by appeal. But about 90

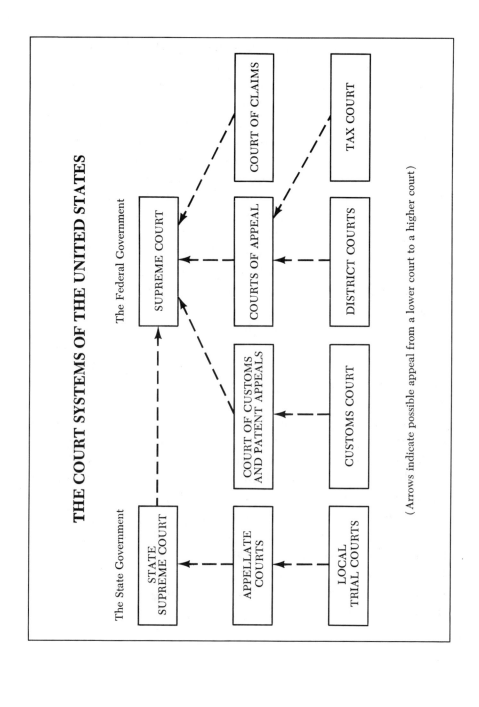

THE COURT SYSTEMS OF THE UNITED STATES

The State Government

The Federal Government

COURT OF CLAIMS

TAX COURT

SUPREME COURT

COURTS OF APPEAL

DISTRICT COURTS

COURT OF CUSTOMS AND PATENT APPEALS

CUSTOMS COURT

STATE SUPREME COURT

APPELLATE COURTS

LOCAL TRIAL COURTS

(Arrows indicate possible appeal from a lower court to a higher court) percent of the cases come on **writs of certiorari** (pronounced *sir-she-oh-*RAY-*ree*). The losing party in the case petitions (asks) the Court for a writ (an order) telling the lower court to send up the record of the case for review.

A very small number of cases come to the Court by other paths. A Court of Appeals may **certify** a case to the Court, asking how to proceed. A person imprisoned in violation of federal law may ask to be released on a writ of **habeas corpus** (a Latin phrase meaning, "You have the body"). The Constitution guarantees the privilege of the writ of habeas corpus as a safeguard of human rights. When a writ is issued, the officer holding a person must show that that person has been lawfully imprisoned.

The Justices consider all the cases submitted to the Court and then vote, in private conferences, on which cases they will review. If four of the nine Justices vote to accept a case, it is put on the Court calendar. The parties involved submit briefs (written arguments). Fewer than 300 cases a year are accepted by the Court. Of these, only about 170 are granted "full review," in which the parties are given a chance to present oral arguments before the Court.

Taking a case to the highest court of the land requires time, and work, and money. Legal papers must be prepared, with forty printed copies for the Justices, the Court's libraries and files, and other uses. Printing and filing fees and the expense of a lawyer can add up to a great deal.

What if a person doesn't have the several thousand or more dollars it may take? That person can apply to the Court **in forma pauperis**—as a poor person. Every year over half the cases filed come in this way. Many are from prisoners who prepare the papers themselves, or sometimes with the help of another prisoner with knowledge of the law. Recent Court rulings have said the states must make law libraries and trained legal personnel available to prisoners.

If an in forma pauperis petition is granted, the Court then pays for printing the legal papers and appoints a lawyer to represent the person bringing the suit. The important case of *Gideon v. Wainwright* (page 39) was submitted in forma pauperis.

Nearly all the cases the Court hears come under its **appellate jurisdiction.** The cases have been appealed to the Court; the Court has the authority to affirm or reverse the lower court's decision. It may also **remand** the case—send it back to the lower court for further proceedings as directed by the Court.

There are just two kinds of cases in which the Court has **original jurisdiction,** where it serves as the trial court. The Constitution provides that the Court try cases involving ambassadors and other foreign diplomats, and cases between states, or between a state and the federal government. These are a very small part of the Court's work.

There are some things the Court won't do. It will not give anyone, even the federal government, an **advisory opinion,** saying what the law would be if this or that came to pass. It won't hear a **friendly suit,** merely for the purpose of testing a law. The opposing parties in a case must be battling for real stakes. Better decisions seem to result when they are made for the purpose of settling actual, not imaginary, controversies.

WHO SERVES ON THE COURT?

The Constitution gives the President the right to appoint the Chief Justice and the Associate Justices of the Court, with the advice and consent of the Senate. Other details of the Court are left to Congress. Congress decides how many justices there should be. The first Court had six. Since 1869, the Court has had nine members—a Chief Justice and eight Associate Justices.

When a Justice resigns, retires, or dies, the President who is then in office selects a new Justice. The name of the nominee is sent to the Senate for approval.

The Constitution lists no requirements for the Justices, but by custom, they have all been United States citizens and have had some background in the law. Presidents may try to choose Justices they hope will support their own general ideas of government; but they are most often careful to select qualified, respected people, and the Senate usually confirms them. When two of President Richard Nixon's nominees were rejected, in 1969 and 1970, they were the first the Senate had refused to confirm in nearly forty years.

If a nominee is rejected, the President names a new candidate. When the Chief Justice's chair is empty, the President may nominate one of the Associate Justices—subject to the Senate's approval—and later fill that Associate's seat; or may select as Chief Justice someone new to the Court, as President Nixon did when he named Warren Burger Chief Justice in 1969.

In the first 190 years of the Supreme Court, there have been only 101 Justices. There has not yet been a woman named to the Court, and Thurgood Marshall, appointed in 1967, was the first black Justice. Most of today's Justices were in their mid-fifties when appointed, and the average age of the Court is now sixty-six.

Some Justices come to the Court from private law offices, or frequently, from the bench of a lower court. Most have been active in politics or have long records of public service. There have been former governors, representatives in Congress, and members of a President's cabinet. One Chief Justice, William Howard Taft, was a former President.

Newly appointed Justices, like all government officials, swear to support and defend the Constitution. They also take a judicial oath, promising to carry out their duties impartially, to "administer justice without respect to persons," and to "do equal right to the poor and to the rich." When a person puts on the black robe and becomes a Justice, party politics and personal interests must be set aside.

THE JUSTICE'S JOB

The Supreme Court Justices spend their working days in the white marble building, which looks like a classical temple, across the plaza from the Capitol. Each Justice has a three-room suite, called "chambers," on the main floor of the building. There is an oak-paneled office with a fireplace, and a bathroom with a shower, and office space for the Justice's staff. Each Justice has a secretary, a messenger, and two, three, or four law clerks. The Chief Justice has a larger staff to handle the additional administrative work of the Chief Justice's office.

Graduating law-school students around the country vie for a position as a Supreme Court Justice's clerk. Justice Horace Gray, in the 1880s, was the first to hire a clerk. That young lawyer's duties included serving as the Justice's barber. Today's clerks usually serve for a year, helping with the vast amount of legal research involved in considering cases and preparing opinions, and in screening appeals. Many law clerks have gone on after the Court to build their own distinguished careers. A number of recent Justices, including Byron White,

William Rehnquist, and John Paul Stevens, once served as law clerks to Supreme Court Justices.

Besides private chambers, the Court building provides the Justices with conference rooms, their own library and reading room (in addition to the main third-floor law library of a quarter of a million books), and a dining room where they may lunch together.

The Justices buy their own black silk robes—the traditional courtroom uniform since colonial days. The court's tallest messenger has the assignment of helping the Justices put the robes on over their street clothes in the robing room next to the courtroom.

The eight Associate Justices earn salaries of $72,000 a year. The Chief Justice, who has some extra duties, receives $75,000 a year. They do pay income tax on these earnings.

Once named to the Supreme Court bench, the Justices hold office "during good behavior." Practically speaking, that means a life term, unless the Justice chooses to retire. A Justice may retire with full pay at age seventy, after ten or more years of service; or at age sixty-five, after fifteen years of service. But the decision to retire is up to the individual Justice.

No Justice has ever been removed. In 1969 Justice Abe Fortas resigned after charges of misconduct, to enable the court to proceed with its work.

The provisions about the Justices' salary and term of office were put in the Constitution so that the judicial branch might be truly independent—not only of the executive and legislative branches, but also of all the various interests that appear before the Court. The justices are free to state their opinions honestly, to judge the cases they hear without any political pressures or concern about their own position. They are independent umpires, able to call the plays as they see them.

Chief Justice Warren E. Burger
administers the presidential oath
of office to Jimmy Carter.

THE COURT SCHEDULE

The Supreme Court year—called its term—officially begins on the first Monday of October. Each term is given the name of the year in which it opens—the 1980 term, for example, began in October, 1980.

The term runs until the Justices have handled all the business before the Court, usually well into June, or even July, of the following year. The term is divided into two-week **sittings,** followed by two-week (or longer) **recesses.** During each sitting, there are public courtroom sessions on Monday, Tuesday, and Wednesday, from 10:00 A.M. to noon, and from 1:00 to 3:00 P.M. At these the Court admits attorneys to practice before it, announces the cases that have been accepted for review or rejected; hands down opinions; and hears oral arguments in the cases before the Court. At each two-week sitting, the Justices hear, usually, twenty-four cases.

Wednesday afternoon after the courtroom sessions and all day Friday are private conference days. The Justices discuss petitions and the cases they have heard argued, and vote on them.

Recess periods are taken up by all the other Court's business. The Justices screen new petitions for review, research and consider current cases, and write their **opinions.** Opinions sum up the facts of a case and then give the Court's decision and the reasons for that decision. The author of the opinion announces it in Court and gives a short summary of the opinion.

By May, the Justices have finished hearing the term's cases. But the Court does not adjourn, or end its term, until the last of its written opinions has been completed and announced.

During the summer recess, the Court's work continues. The Justices take it with them wherever they go. Every week there are new petitions for review; and vast amounts of reading and preparation for the cases coming up in the next term.

A DAY IN THE SUPREME COURT

Every year, more than half a million people visit the Supreme Court. The building is open to the public every day, Monday through Friday, except holidays, from 9:00 A.M. to 4:30 P.M. When the Court is in session, visitors can listen to the proceedings in the courtroom, although they sometimes have to wait until there are seats available. If the Court is not sitting, there are guided tours of the courtroom.

The gleaming white marble structure has been the Court's home since it was completed in 1935. Before that, the Court met in makeshift quarters. The first two sessions, in 1790, were held on the second floor of the Royal Exchange building in New York City. When the capital was moved to Philadelphia in 1791, the Court moved too, and met in Liberty Hall, and then Old City Hall. The Court followed the capital again in 1801 when it moved to Washington, and the Court used borrowed rooms in the Capitol building until it was provided with its own permanent home.

The building's impressive columned entrance is crowned with an inscription that is a reminder of the special responsibility of the Court: "Equal Justice Under Law." Below, bronze doors open into the Great Hall. At the end of this corridor is the courtroom. Marble walls and columns, rich mahogany furniture, deep-red curtains and floor coverings, and a carved ceiling provide a majestic setting for the highest court in the land. Above the stately columns, on the four sides of the chamber, are sculptured panels that show a procession of historic lawgivers, including Hammurabi, Moses, Solomon, Confucius, Mohammed, Napoleon, and John Marshall, the eminent nineteenth-century Chief Justice.

Just inside the courtroom is the public seating section, with benches and chairs for about 300 visitors. A bronze rail separates this section from areas reserved for the press—newspaper, television, and radio reporters—and for members of the bar—lawyers—who want to listen to the oral arguments, and guests of the Justices. Next, there are tables for the lawyers who are scheduled to argue before the Court. White goose-feather quills on each table are reminders of the Court's early days. They are usually taken by the lawyers, who may not have another chance to appear in this courtroom.

At the end of the chamber the Justices' bench, or desk, rises 4 feet (1.2 m) from the floor against a backdrop of marble columns and velvet curtains. The Marshal of the Court, who serves as business manager and director of security, has a desk at one end of the bench. At the other end there is a desk for the Clerk of the Court, who supervises all the Court's papers and procedures.

Nine upholstered black chairs of uneven height wait behind the bench. When the building was first opened, the Justices were presented with tall wooden chairs, handsomely carved and exactly alike. These were so uncomfortable that the Court members went on sitting in the chairs they liked. Now, the Justices choose from several types of chairs when they join the Court.

As the Court day is about to begin, at 10 A.M., visitors are seated by the Marshal and the Marshal's aides; the court messengers place paper and pencils at each Justice's place. They are usually college or law students. During the Court

[18]

The Courtroom

session they pass messages from one Justice to another, find staff members when they are needed, get books from the library, and run other errands.

At 10 A.M. a gavel falls and everyone stands. The velvet curtains are parted, and the robed Justices come out to take their places.

The Court Crier chants, "The Honorable, the Chief Justice and the Associate Justices of the Supreme Court of the United States." After the Justices have moved to their places, the Crier continues, "Oyez! Oyez! Oyez!" ("Oyez" means "Hear ye!") "All persons having business before the Honorable, the Supreme Court of the United States, are admonished to draw near and give their attention, for the Court is now sitting. God save the United States and this Honorable Court."

Another gavel blow is the signal for everyone to sit. At the middle of the bench is the Chief Justice. The other Justices sit by order of seniority, or length of service on the Court. The two most senior associates sit next to the Chief Justice, one on each side. The newest Justices are at the ends of the bench. When a Justice leaves, all the chairs are moved—except that of the Chief Justice. The new member sits at the end.

The first business of the court day may be to issue a list of Court actions, and then admit attorneys to the bar of the Court. Once admitted, they may argue cases before the Court. If any opinions are ready to be released, they are then announced.

The rest of the Court day is devoted to hearing cases. There is no jury, and no witnesses are called. This is a lawyers' court. Cases come here from the lower courts for final decision by the Justices. The written arguments—briefs—have already been given to the Justices. This is the lawyers' one chance to speak their piece and present their strongest arguments. Generally, each side is allowed a half-hour to speak. The Justices may interrupt with questions whenever they want.

When the lawyer's time is nearly up, a white warning light flashes on the reading desk where the lawyer stands. When a red light flashes, the time has expired and the lawyer sits down.

In the early days of the Court, lawyers wore formal clothes. Daniel Webster would appear in a long blue coat with brass buttons. Chief Justice Taft once sent a lawyer home to put on a vest. Today, only some government attorneys and a few others wear formal cutaway coats and morning trousers. Most wear business clothes.

After the one-hour noon recess, the Court resumes where it left off. One case follows right after another until the court day is over at 3:00 P.M. exactly. Grover Cleveland, a former President, once was arguing a case at the end of the day. He told Chief Justice Melville W. Fuller, whom he had appointed when he was President, that he would be finished in two minutes. "Mr. Cleveland," said the Chief Justice courteously, "we will hear you tomorrow morning."

HOW CASES ARE DECIDED

After the case is heard in the courtroom, the hardest part of the Justices' work begins. Working from the case records, the lawyers' briefs and arguments, and the whole history of the law, each Justice has to reach a decision on what is the law of the case.

Almost every Friday during the term, the Justices meet in their oak-paneled conference room to discuss and vote on the cases they have heard. The conference is completely private and everything is kept secret. No outsiders are allowed to enter. The junior Justice acts as doorkeeper to take messages.

As the Justices file into the room at 9:30 Friday morning, each shakes hands with all the others. (The custom is observed too when they gather to go on the bench on hearing days.) This "conference handshake"—dating from Chief Justice Fuller's time at the end of the nineteenth century—is a reminder that no matter how much the Justices may disagree in their views, they share a "harmony of aims."

The conference continues late into the afternoon—until all the 100 or 120 items on the day's agenda, or order of business, have been considered. They discuss and vote on the requests for Court review that are before them, and take up consideration of the cases they have heard argued during that week's courtroom sessions. Usually twelve cases are heard during the three days (Monday, Tuesday, and Wednesday) of hearings. Recently, an extra conference session has been added on Wednesday afternoons, after the 3:00 P.M. close of the courtroom hearing. The Justices use this session to consider some cases and lighten their load at the Friday conference.

The Justices work on one case right after another, with just a short break for lunch. The Chief Justice begins the discussion of each case with a summary of the facts and an analysis of the law in the case. The Chief Justice then usually tells how he thinks he will vote.

Next the senior Associate Justice, and then the other Justices by order of seniority, give their views. After the discussion—which is sometimes long and heated—the Chief Justice calls for a vote. The order of seniority is reversed now, and the newest Justice votes first, so that the senior Justices won't be too strong an influence. The decision is determined by a majority vote.

Since the Justices know the law, it might seem that they would agree on decisions. And, sometimes, decisions are unanimous. But the law is usually not that simple—if it were, we would do without judges, Justice Felix Frankfurter said. The information could be fed into a computer, and the decision would be produced. A judge starts by trying to match the case with earlier ones that have been decided according to rules of law. When the colors don't match, a judge's work really begins, Justice Benjamin Cardozo said. Many cases involve more than one principle of law and, often, a number of different interests.

After the vote, one Justice is assigned the task of writing the majority opinion. That Justice must present the decision, explain the law involved, and give the reasons why the Justices decided as they did. If the Chief Justice voted with the majority, he assigns the opinion to himself, or one of the Justices who voted with him. If the Chief Justice voted with the minority, the senior Justice voting with the majority makes the assignment.

Writing the opinion begins with weeks or even months of research, thought, and analysis. The Justice outlines the ideas, then writes a first draft. Law clerks work closely with the Justice to help through these stages. The draft is sent to a printing shop on the ground floor of the Court building, under tight security to prevent any leaks of information.

All the Justices receive copies of the draft of the opinion. They send the author comments, suggestions, and criticisms. They meet, argue, debate, and sometimes change their votes. The author of the opinion makes changes and may prepare as many as ten drafts, but it is not always possible to get the Justices to agree on wording or on some points of an opinion.

When the Justices have finished reviewing it, and all the changes have been made, the opinion is voted on at a conference. After the final form is accepted, a summary of it is read in Court by the author. Some of the Justices who voted for the decision but have different reasons write their own concurring, or agreeing, opinions.

Once a decision is announced, or handed down, it becomes the law. The decision must be obeyed; it is binding on the parties in the case. And the reasoning of the opinion becomes a part of the body of law of the land. Lawyers will use it in arguing future cases; judges will base decisions on it.

The Justices in the minority—those who do not agree with the decision—choose from among themselves one Justice to explain their views in a dissenting opinion, or dissent. Sometimes a number of Justices write dissents, to present their own views. The dissents are announced in Court and are an important part of the record. They provide criticism of the majority opinion and are thus a safeguard of our constitutional system. Sometime, in later cases, a dissent can be the basis of a different opinion, or even a reversal of the earlier opinion. As time passes, public attitudes and beliefs change and the world itself changes; new Justices are named, and the Court changes too.

Can the Supreme Court make its decisions stick? That was settled in 1824, when an Ohio state official lost a tax case in the Supreme Court but refused to return $120,000. The federal courts went into action. A United States marshal jailed the official for contempt of court, took a key from the official's pocket, and removed the money from the state treasury—all by due process of law.

In 1957, President Dwight Eisenhower told the nation, "The very basis of our individual rights and freedoms rests upon the certainty that the President and the executive branch of government will support and ensure the carrying out of the decisions of the federal courts."

A CONTINUING
CONSTITUTIONAL CONVENTION

The United States Constitution is a short document. It has only about 7,000 words and can be read aloud in forty minutes. At first look, it seems clear and straightforward.

The President, it says, shall hold "office during the term of four years." Neither a state nor the United States shall "grant any title of nobility."

But there may be more here than it first appears. No person shall "be deprived of life, liberty, or property, without due process of law." If we look up the phrase "due process of law" in the dictionary, we read, "that course of legal proceedings that is in accordance with the law of the land." "The law of the land," in the United States, is a great body of statute, precedent, history, custom, and interpretation that can be traced back to Magna Carta—the charter of rights King John of England was forced to grant his subjects in 1215. Perhaps a dictionary is not enough help in trying to understand the Constitution.

The Government Printing Office in Washington, D.C., will sell and mail to any interested person *The Constitution of the United States of America: Analysis and Interpretation*. This large volume, prepared by the Library of Congress, discusses each phrase of the Constitution (the discussion of "due process" takes nearly 200 pages) and sums up briefly what the Supreme Court has ruled in cases involving the Constitution. At the end of every Court term a supplement is issued, to add the Court's new rulings to those of previous years.

This short document then—the Constitution—is not all there is to know about the basis of the government. Chief Justice John Marshall, whose leadership helped mold the Court into a vigorous and equal branch of government, said that the Constitution provides the "great outlines" of our government. But the details were left to be filled in. As Marshall wrote: "We must never forget it is a *constitution* we are expounding. . . . intended to endure for ages to come, and consequently, to be adapted to the various crises of human affairs."

The Supreme Court sits every year as a continuing constitutional convention—to fill in the details, to adapt the Constitution to today's crises. It is the Court's responsibility to mark out the boundaries between the power of the states and the nation, the President and Congress, and the individual citizen and the government.

The Supreme Court's opinions are published in *The United States Reports.* They now fill over 445 volumes. Law libraries in county courthouses usually have them available for anyone who is interested in reading some. The next sections of this book discuss some of the important areas of concern for the Supreme Court—areas where the Court's decisions have shaped and influenced American life.

THE PRESIDENT AND CONGRESS

The Supreme Court has the power to declare an action of the President, or a law passed by Congress, to be unconstitutional. This is part of the system of checks and balances that is built

*On exhibit in the Court building
are various things used by
Chief Justice John Marshall.
In the background is a painting of
"The Great Chief Justice,"
completed in 1834 when he was 79.*

into the Constitution. If one branch of government goes too far, assumes too much power, another branch can check or balance it.

During the Korean War, when a steelworkers' strike seemed near, President Harry Truman sent army personnel into the mills to keep them running. The Court ruled that his seizure of the mills was illegal. They said he had no power to do this on his own; it was a job for the nation's lawmakers.

In 1974 the Supreme Court ruled that President Richard Nixon would have to release his tape recordings of conversations with his aides that had been called for as evidence in a criminal trial. This "battle for the tapes," *United States* v. *Nixon,* was part of the Watergate burglary and cover-up scandal that led to President Nixon's resignation. The Court ruled that it, not the President, had the final say on the meaning of the Constitution. Chief Justice Burger repeated Justice Marshall's famous phrase: "It is emphatically the province and duty of the judicial department to say what the law is."

Congress too may be stopped by the Court. In 1974 the Court overturned a law that had extended the minimum wage requirements of federal law to people employed by state or local governments. The Court said Congress did not have the right to legislate over the states in this matter. It had exceeded its powers.

The Court has not often used this power to review the acts of the President or of Congress. Only a few more than a hundred acts of Congress have been declared unconstitutional, out of the over 40,000 public laws that have been enacted. But the fact that the Court has this power, and has used it, has been an important influence on the people who prepare and enact legislation, and on the executive branch.

*The great bronze doors
at the main west entrance.*

Chicago once made a river run backwards. Through miracles of engineering, the Chicago River was turned away from Lake Michigan. Boats sailed across Illinois and down the Mississippi to New Orleans. The city tapped Lake Michigan for water, and flushed its sewage into the Mississippi River.

Then came the complications. Down went the lake's water level. Docks and warehouses farther north were left high and dry. Fishing grounds disappeared. Shoreline homes stared at mud flats. Wisconsin and Michigan sued Illinois for letting Chicago take the water. Several other states joined in.

When one state has a disagreement with another, the dispute is taken directly to the Supreme Court for trial. In this case, *Wisconsin* v. *Illinois* (1930), the Court ruled that Chicago was entitled to enough water for navigation, but no more. However, the people's health was protected. The city was allowed eight years in which to build sewage treatment plants. Meanwhile, its water ration was gradually reduced.

Even today boundary disputes between states are still being brought before the Court. Ohio and Kentucky had quarreled for years over the Ohio River border between the states. In 1980 the Court ruled that the river's low-water mark in 1792—when Kentucky was admitted to the union—should determine the boundary, rather than the low-water mark of today.

THE COMMERCE CLAUSE

The Constitution gives Congress the power to regulate "commerce" with foreign nations and among the states. It also gives

Congress the power to make whatever laws are "necessary and proper" to enable the federal government to use its other powers.

When the Constitution was written, no one was really sure what these phrases meant. Then, in the case of *Gibbons* v. *Ogden* (1824), the "Steamboat Case," the Supreme Court under John Marshall had a chance to interpret them. Gibbons wanted to carry passengers from New Jersey to New York in his steamboat, but Ogden's group alone had a license from New York State to operate in its waters. Gibbons won the case. Closing New York Harbor to competing steamboats and allowing only Ogden to carry passengers would interfere with commerce between the states, said the Court.

In the opinion, the term "commerce" was given a broad, or general, meaning. Marshall wrote that it covers more than just buying and selling—it means every kind of business dealing, including navigation and the means and routes of transportation. Regulating interstate commerce is the responsibility of Congress, he said.

When Congress makes rules for commerce between the states, it is said to use the **commerce power.** Supreme Court rulings through the years have brought all kinds of dealings that involve more than one state within this power—not only buying, selling, and navigation, but the tariff, railroads, electricity, pipelines, the telephone and telegraph, manufacturing, mining, agriculture, radio, television, and airborne commerce. Since the 1930s, the Court's broad interpretation of the commerce power has allowed Congress to regulate child labor, minimum wages, racial discrimination in public accommodations, and other matters that affect interstate commerce.

The states need money for roads, schools, and all the expenses of local government. And the Supreme Court upholds their right to lay taxes that are fair to all and not too much of a burden on the nation's commerce. But the Court can and does declare some taxation illegal. A laundry in Memphis, Tennessee, sent ten trucks into Mississippi to pick up and deliver bundles. Mississippi slapped a $50 tax on each truck, although laundries located in Mississippi paid only $8. The Court ruled this illegal. In a similar 1979 ruling, the Court held that New Mexico could not legally tax electricity generated within the state and sold to out-of-state consumers at a higher rate than it taxed electricity sold within the state. The Court has thrown out many laws like this. If allowed to stand, such taxes would lead to tax wars. Soon every state would put up tariff walls against its neighbors.

Other tax cases are more complicated. How do you tax railroad cars that are here today and gone tomorrow, or a plane that streaks across the state in thirty minutes? States have tried various ways. In case of dispute, the Supreme Court decides whether the tax is fair to all concerned—to the state, to the company, and to other states in which the company does business.

Some trucks carry registration plates from several states. A fee is paid for each plate—a sort of state tax for wear and tear on the highways. Some states limit the size and weight of trucks, or make them use certain roads. The Court has held that a state can make rules like these under the **police power.** This phrase means something different from the power of the state police. It means a state's broad power to protect the people's health, safety, and welfare. But the police power has limits. Illinois told one trucking line to keep out of the state entirely, and the Supreme Court said that interfered with the federal government's interstate commerce rules.

When a state's police power and the nation's commerce power meet head on, the Court asks: Which has the greater interest here, the state or the nation? Did Congress intend to regulate this kind of commerce or to let the states do it? Does the state law help or hinder the federal law? Perhaps there is room for both.

Because of the federal commerce power, we can cross the continent without passports and do business everywhere within the United States. We have supermarkets, network shows, mass production, and high living standards. Yet we are not under the rule of one all-powerful goverment, for most everyday affairs come within the police power of state and local governments. The federal Union rests on balanced powers like these. And the Supreme Court is the balance wheel.

PROPERTY RIGHTS
VERSUS SOCIAL WELFARE

Words are sometimes given different meanings in different times, or under different circumstances. The Constitution's Fifth Amendment says that no person shall be "deprived of life, liberty, or property, without due process of law." Americans of the year 1800 might have explained that as, "it means they can't hang, jail, or fine you without a fair trial."

As the years passed, many people grew to feel that the due process guarantee was concerned mostly with property rights—that it protected them from having their property taken without a fair hearing. This belief was bolstered by the 1857 Supreme Court decision in the case of *Dred Scott* v. *Sandford*. The Court, under Chief Justice Roger B. Taney, ruled that the black slave Dred Scott was still a slave after living on free soil. A slave was property, said Taney, and to take away an owner's property "could hardly be dignified with the name of due process of law."

After the Civil War, the federal government guarantees

[33]

of the Fifth Amendment were made binding on the states by the Fourteenth Amendment. Former slaves became citizens, but the interpretation of "due process" remained a product of the time and circumstances. Property and economic rights were still emphasized over human rights. In 1905 the Court ruled against a New York law that had called for a ten-hour limit to the working day in bakeries. In *Lochner* v. *New York* the Court called the law "meddlesome," and said it took away bakery workers' liberty without due process of law—their liberty to make their own working contracts with their employers.

In 1916, Congress passed a law forbidding goods made by children under fourteen to be traded between the states. The Court struck down this law too, in *Hammer* v. *Dagenhart* (1918). It said the law interfered with matters properly left to the states.

But if the Court was not yet ready to make rulings for the protection of people over property, at least one of its Justices was—Oliver Wendell Holmes, sometimes called the Great Dissenter. His dissenting opinions in these two cases are among the most famous in the Court's history. Holmes pointed out that liberty to do as one likes is interfered with by school laws and many other laws, and that a reasonable person might consider the bakery law proper on the score of health. As for the child labor law, Holmes claimed it did not meddle with anything belonging to the states. They might do as they liked at home, he said, but when they sent the product of ruined lives across the state line, they were no longer within their rights.

In 1908 a most unusual brief was filed with the Court in support of Oregon's ten-hour maximum working day for women. A page or two of law was followed by a hundred pages of medical opinions regarding the harm done women by long hours of factory work. It won the case, and a brief like this is still called a **Brandeis brief** for Louis D. Brandeis, who prepared it.

Justice Brandeis (left, standing)
and Justice Holmes (second from right, seated)
pose with other members of the Court in 1917.

Brandeis was later a Justice, and he and Holmes frequently worked together to try to lead the Court to recognize that the law should develop and change along with the needs of the society it serves. In the 1920s, these two brilliant Justices opened the path to what has been called the Constitutional Revolution of 1937. Here the Court's main emphasis changed from the protection of economic interests and property rights, to a concern for public welfare.

The case of Elsie Parrish, a hotel chambermaid, was one of the first in this new era. She sued for $14.50 a week under the Washington state minimum-wage law. Her employer replied that the law took away his liberty to make a contract, without due process of law, and he quoted the Supreme Court to prove it. But America was digging out of a depression, and the Court had changed. Chief Justice Hughes said reasonable regulation of wages *was* due process of law. He thought the liberty that mattered most to Elsie Parrish was the kind that protected her health and welfare.

Other Court decisions soon followed, letting the federal government tackle great national problems under the commerce power. Among them were flood control, the marketing of crops, and collective bargaining between employers and wage-earners.

Thus the Court came to serve as a balance between individual property rights and the welfare of society as a whole.

LIBERTY VERSUS AUTHORITY

The big car screeched to a halt at the McNabb settlement in the Tennessee mountains.

Four men jumped out. "All right, boys, federal officers!"

Branches crashed underfoot, shadowy figures melted away, and all was still.

The revenuers began tipping over cans of moonshine whiskey. Suddenly a boulder landed at Officer Leeper's feet. He went after the culprit, flashlight in hand. As he searched the family burying ground, a shot came from the darkness and he fell, mortally wounded.

Who of that numerous mountain clan had pulled the trigger? It was hard to say. The officers dragged two brothers and a cousin from hiding and took them to Chattanooga, 12 miles (19.3 km) away. The McNabb boys had never before been that far from home. They had quit school in the third grade, and they had no lawyer to advise them. After being questioned all night and all day, they signed "confessions" and were speedily convicted.

What chance of a fair hearing did the three McNabbs have against the power of the United States? The answer is in *McNabb* v. *United States,* where the Supreme Court decided against the convictions and spoke out for "civilized standards of procedure."

We are reminded in the Court's opinion that an accused person has the constitutional right to be taken promptly before a judge, who may release the person on bail or dismiss the charges. This procedure guards against the "third degree" and forced confessions. It discourages "easy but self-defeating ways in which brutality is substituted for brains as an instrument of crime detection."

The Court attaches much importance to the rights of people accused of a crime, and the procedures by which these rights are protected. "The history of liberty has largely been the history of observance of procedural safeguards," says the McNabb opinion. Five of the ten amendments in the Constitution's **Bill of Rights** deal with **procedural rights.** Among them are the right to have a lawyer, to face one's accusers in open court, to have a speedy and public trial, and to be tried by an impartial jury.

The Fourth Amendment protects people from unreasonable searches and seizures, or arrests. Government officers must go before a judge and get a warrant (court order) allowing them to conduct a search, or to seize a person or property. In a decision announced in 1980 (*Payton* v. *New York*), the Court expressly stated that police must have warrants to enter people's homes to make an arrest. In the decision Justice John Paul Stevens wrote: ". . . the Fourth Amendment has drawn a firm line at the entrance to the house. . . . that threshold may not reasonably be crossed without a warrant."

The Court has also said, in *Katz* v. *United States* (1967), that the Fourth Amendment protects people from the government's use of wiretaps or other listening devices. The Court said these were searches, and unless a warrant had been obtained, any evidence gained came from an illegal search, and could not be used.

Under the Fifth Amendment, people cannot be forced to be witnesses against themselves. The Court has interpreted this to mean they have the right to remain silent. This privilege against self-incrimination was won, said Justice William O. Douglas, in the long struggle to be safe from torture. The privilege also protects innocent people who might come under suspicion because of unusual circumstances.

In a ruling that has become part of every police officer's training, the Court reinforced this right. In *Miranda* v. *Arizona* (1966), the Court ruled that before questioning suspects, the police must warn them that their statements may be used as evidence against them, and advise them of their right to remain silent, and their right to an attorney. Without these formal warnings, and the suspect's waiver of these rights, any statement made by a suspect cannot be used as evidence.

Every person accused of a crime is guaranteed the "assistance of counsel" by the Sixth Amendment. But sometimes the person on trial is too poor to hire a lawyer. For many years, courts had held that the state must provide a lawyer if the person was accused of a crime punishable by death. In a case that affirms the promise of "equal justice," the Court extended this protection. In *Gideon* v. *Wainwright* (1963), the Court ruled that every poor defendant in any state criminal trial had the right to a lawyer appointed by the court.

The Eighth Amendment protects people accused of a crime from "cruel or unusual punishment." In nineteenth-century America punishments were generally harsher than they are today; and capital punishment, or the death penalty, was accepted as just punishment for some crimes.

Over the years, ideas have changed and people have argued for the abolition or limitation of the death penalty. In 1972 the Court heard a group of cases (called by the lead case, *Furman* v. *Georgia*) and ruled that the death penalty in these cases constituted cruel and unusual punishment in violation of the Eighth and Fourteenth Amendments. They said the penalty was inconsistently and arbitrarily imposed, and thereby unfair. Thirty-five states then enacted new death penalty laws that they thought would satisfy the Court's objections. Five of these were tested by the Court in 1976; three were upheld and two rejected. Thus the Court has said the death penalty is constitutional, but the states must establish fair and precise guidelines for its use.

Are these amendments and the other provisions of the Bill of Rights binding on the states, too? Yes, the Court has ruled.

[39]

All of the Bill of Rights' provisions have been found to apply to the states. When the Court ruled in 1969 that the constitutional guarantee against double jeopardy (being tried more than once for the same crime) applied to the states, this was the last of the provisions to be tested. And some Justices consider the "due process" clause of the Fourteenth Amendment a guarantee of the whole Bill of Rights. However, the Court has said that a state may follow other procedures if they still provide the fundamentals of a fair trial. For example, a state may try certain cases with a jury of less than twelve.

THE COURT AND THE FIRST AMENDMENT

Freedom of religion, free speech, a free press, and the right of assembly and petition—these fundamental freedoms guaranteed the people by the First Amendment to the Constitution— are often the issues in the most significant cases brought before the Court. And the rulings in individual cases sometimes have had far-reaching effects, and become part of our legacy of freedom.

Newton Cantwell and his two sons were members of the religious group Jehovah's Witnesses. While offering religious books for sale in New Haven, Connecticut, they were arrested. The charge was soliciting without a certificate from the state public welfare council. This council had the power to approve religious causes—it could grant permission to solicit to one group and refuse another. The Court ruled that a state cannot pick and choose among religions, but must treat them all in the same way. *Cantwell* v. *Connecticut* (1940) has become a foundation stone of religious liberty.

[40]

Besides forbidding interference with any religion, the Constitution also bars any law establishing a religion. In *Engel* v. *Vitale* (1962), the "School Prayer Case," the Court ruled that no government could prescribe an official prayer to be used in school. The following year the Court reinforced this ruling. In *Arlington Township School District* v. *Schempp*, it said the state cannot require students to recite the Lord's Prayer or read from the Bible, since these practices violate the "establishment of religion" clause of the First Amendment.

The words of Justice Oliver Wendell Holmes are often quoted as an explanation of the privilege of free speech. He would say that to many people free speech means, "You may say anything that I don't think shocking." But the real test of free speech, he added, is "freedom for the thought we hate." Justice Holmes did feel that there might sometimes have to be restrictions on the freedom of speech; for example, he observed, a person could not be allowed to shout "Fire!" in a crowded theater.

From the Court's earliest days to the present, it has been often asked to rule on issues of freedom of speech and the press. Specific cases reflect the concerns of the time. So in 1969 the Court ruled, in *Tinker* v. *Des Moines Independent Community School District*, that the free speech doctrine gave students the right to wear black armbands to school as a protest against United States involvement in the Vietnam War. In 1964, in *New York Times* v. *Sullivan*, the Court protected the right of the press (and the public) to criticize public officials. And in 1971, in *New York Times* v. *United States*, the Court allowed newspapers to publish a secret government study of United States involvement in Southeast Asia—the "Pentagon Papers"—under the First Amendment guarantee of a free press.

Free speech, a free press, and the other freedoms may

have hard sledding in difficult times. They are attacked from many sides, and there are frequent attempts to limit them. The Court has tried to keep a delicate balance between liberty and authority; but its decisions have often stirred up controversy and anger. Cases about libel, obscenity, censorship, the expression of unpopular views, national security, and other matters raise important questions for the Court and for the people.

THE COURT AND CIVIL RIGHTS

A look at some of the Court's decisions on issues of civil, or human, rights—the rights and freedoms of individuals—throughout the Court's history provides clear evidence of how the Court and the nation itself have shifted in attitudes and beliefs.

In 1857 the Court said, in the Dred Scott decision, that black slaves were not and could not be citizens. But eleven years later, in 1868, the Fourteenth Amendment to the Constitution extended the rights of citizenship to former slaves. Still, these new rights were limited. In *Plessy* v. *Ferguson* (1896) the Court upheld a Louisiana law that provided for separate, or segregated, railroad cars for blacks and whites. The Court ruled that "separate but equal" facilities were legal.

This "separate but equal" doctrine remained the law for over fifty years, until the historic case of *Brown* v. *Board of Education of Topeka* (1954). Linda Brown was a young black schoolgirl. By long custom, she had been assigned to a separate school with other black students. Suits had been brought on behalf of Linda and pupils in other states, asking that they be admitted to schools reserved for white students.

Chief Justice Earl Warren announced the Court's unanimous decision. Calling education "the very foundation of good citizenship," he said it is "a right which must be made available to all on equal terms." The Court concluded that "separate educational facilities are inherently unequal," and that children like Linda were being "deprived of the equal protection of the laws guaranteed by the Fourteenth Amendment."

In the years following there have been many other decisions to ensure equal opportunity in the nation's schools. The Court said that a judge may order specific plans for school desegregation; that methods such as busing of students and setting up of new school districts to do away with segregation are acceptable. The faculty and staffs of schools were to be integrated. Segregated private schools were told that if they refused to admit black students, they might be violating the students' civil rights.

Beyond school desegregation, the Court moved into other areas too—to provide guarantees of civil rights and equal protection of the law for all Americans. It upheld laws barring discrimination in hotels and other public facilities; it ruled on questions of voting rights, discrimination in housing and in employment, and protected workers' job rights.

Today there are new kinds of civil rights issues before the Court: women's rights; the rights of the aged, the feeble, and dependent children; and the rights of those who say they have been discriminated against because of advantages offered to minority group members.

Special programs and other forms of help for racial minorities, women, and other victims of past discrimination have led to charges of "reverse discrimination." Allan Bakke, a white man who was refused admission to medical school, claimed that he was a victim of racial discrimination. In admitting new stu-

*A long line of people wait for
admission to the Court to hear the arguments in
Allan Bakke's suit against the University of California's
special admissions program for the disadvantaged.*

dents, the school reserved a certain number of places for minority group members. But Bakke's test marks were higher than those of the minority students admitted under the program. The Court's ruling, in *Regents of the University of California* v. *Bakke,* in June, 1978, did not give a clear answer as to how much help "affirmative action" programs can provide. The Court said Bakke must be judged as an individual by the state-supported institution, and therefore must be admitted. But it also said that the University had the right to maintain an affirmative action program that considered race as one factor in the selection of students.

The following June, 1979, the Court rejected a challenge to another affirmative action plan, in *United Steelworkers of America* v. *Weber.* A white worker who had been left out of a training program while black workers with less seniority were included, brought a suit for racial discrimination. The Court decided that private employers can give special treatment to black workers to get rid of "racial imbalance" in jobs that have been traditionally held by white workers only.

FROM MARSHALL TO BURGER

The Supreme Court is sometimes called by the name of its Chief Justice, as was the Marshall Court, led by the "great" Chief Justice, John Marshall, from 1801 to 1835.

When Marshall came onto the Court, it was neither strong nor influential, and had few cases to hear. The first Chief Justice, John Jay, had chosen to resign to become governor of New York. Marshall, during his thirty-four–year term, helped shape the Court into a powerful branch of government.

[45]

In modern days, the Warren Court was an active and forceful agent that affected many aspects of American life. Under Earl Warren, the Chief Justice from 1954 to 1969, the Court emerged as the protector of the Constitutional rights of the citizens. Its rulings on school desegregation, equal opportunity, voting rights, legislative redistricting, and the separation of church and state fostered great changes in American society.

The Burger Court, under Warren Burger who was named Chief Justice in 1969, has not created as clear an image. It has faced many new kinds of challenges and, like the Warren Court, has often stirred controversy. It limited the death penalty and overturned laws barring abortions. It allowed the publication of the "Pentagon Papers," extended attacks on segregated schools, and supported equal rights for men and women. It has also put limits on the rights of the accused and on the freedom of the press.

Through the nation's history, the Court has been responsive to the people. At times it has led the way, but more often it has reflected society—its concerns, interests, and attitudes.

THE COURT'S SECRET WEAPON

Umpires are not always popular, and neither is the Supreme Court. In every case it decides, there is a loser.

"Our people often criticize the Court and disagree with it, but they have a respect and reverence for it, born of decades of experience," Justice William O. Douglas told an audience in India.

The Court has weathered every storm, including controversies with Presidents as popular as Jefferson, Jackson,

The Burger Court in 1976.
From left: seated, Associate Justices Byron R. White,
William J. Brennan, Jr.; Chief Justice Warren E. Burger;
Associate Justices Potter Stewart, Thurgood Marshall;
standing, Associate Justices William H. Rehnquist,
Harry A. Blackmun, Lewis F. Powell, Jr., John P. Stevens.

Lincoln, and the two Roosevelts. Its prestige has grown through the years.

The Court has been placed beyond the reach of day-by-day politics, as Justice Robert H. Jackson once pointed out, so that it can stand guard over fundamental rights without depending on the outcome of elections. It protects the rights of all people, on all sides of every public question.

Justice Hugo L. Black said, "No higher duty, no more solemn responsibility, rests upon this Court, than that of translating into living law and maintaining this constitutional shield deliberately planned and inscribed for the benefit of every human being subject to our Constitution. . . ."

Supreme Court Justices go to great lengths to avoid even the appearance of partiality. They **disqualify** themselves from sitting in cases if they have any possible interest in the outcome. Once, Chief Justice Harlan F. Stone owned shares of stock in a company that was charged with breaking the antitrust laws. He promptly sold his holdings and put the money into another company. Soon this company, too, was in trouble. The Chief Justice then sold his stock a second time, so that he could vote his beliefs with a clear conscience, if later he sat in judgment on the case.

When umpires rule a hometown player out at third base, the crowd may yell that they need glasses. Over the long pull, though, umpires command respect if people know they are impartial.

So actually the Supreme Court's authority rests less on force than on its reputation for fairness. Justice Douglas wrote that the strength of the Court "is in the command it has over the hearts and minds of the people." We look to the Court as the highest source of the law of the land.

adjourn—to postpone or suspend a court session

advisory opinion—an opinion stating what the law would be in a possible situation; such opinions are never given by the Supreme Court

affirm—to declare a lower court's decision correct

amicus curiae—Latin for "friend of the court": a person who, as an interested party, presents views in a brief or an oral argument

appeal—a request from the losing party in a suit that a decision be reviewed by a higher court

appellant—one who appeals a case to a higher court

appellate (or appeals) court—a court that reviews a lower court's proceedings and hears appeals from its decisions

appellee—one against whom an appeal is taken; the winner in the lower court

attorney general—the highest officer in the Department of Justice

bail—money or other security put up to free a person under arrest and guarantee the person's appearance for trial. The Eighth Amendment forbids excessive bail

bill of attainder—a law that pronounces a person guilty of a crime without a trial. Under Article I of the Constitution, neither the federal government nor any state may pass a bill of attainder

Bill of Rights—the first ten amendments to the Constitution. They limit the power of the federal government over individual citizens and over the states

Brandeis brief—a legal brief describing medical, sociological, and other background factors in a case; first used by Louis Brandeis

brief—a written argument submitted to a court, presenting the facts of the case and the reasons supporting the submittor's position

calendar—a list of cases set down for argument, in the order in which they will be called

case—an action in court to protect rights or redress wrongs

certify—to send a Court of Appeals case to the Supreme Court, asking for instructions

certiorari, writ of (*sir-she-oh-*RAY-*ree*)—from a short form of Latin words meaning "we wish to be informed"; an order to a lower court to send up the record of a case for review

chambers—a judge's private office

civil case—one involving a dispute between persons, persons and governments, or governments; not a criminal case

civil law—a system of law growing out of Roman law and the Napoleonic Code, and followed in Europe and Louisiana. "Civil" does not mean the same here as in "civil case" above

commerce power—Congress' constitutional power "to regulate commerce with foreign nations, and among the several states, and with the Indian tribes." By Supreme Court decisions, it includes commerce within a state which is mixed with interstate commerce

common law—a system of law in England in the late Middle Ages, and since then shaped by court decisions in English-speaking countries and in our various states. In different senses, common law is contrasted with civil or Roman law; with statutory law as passed by legislative bodies; and with equity (see below)

concurring opinion—one agreeing with the result of another in the same case, but stating the reasons separately

constitutional—agreeing with the Constitution; as, a law not in violation of its provisions. A constitutional government is one whose powers are limited by a constitution

constitutional law—principles that guide the Supreme Court in fixing the boundaries of the authority belonging to different branches of the government and to the states and the nation; and in balancing the interests of private property and social welfare and of the individual and the government

construction—the process of finding out the meaning of a constitutional provision

contempt—disregard of a court's authority, or disobedience of its lawful orders. Refusal to answer the proper questions of a congressional committee is "contempt of Congress"

counsel—the lawyer or lawyers in a case; also the advice they give

court below—the lower court in which a case was last heard

court-martial—a trial in the armed forces under the Uniform Code of Military Justice

Court of Appeals—a federal appellate court in one of the eleven circuits of the United States. It stands between the District Courts and the Supreme Court

criminal case—one in which the defendant is charged with breaking a law intended to protect the public from injury

decision—a judgment, or what a court decides, in settling a case, as when the Supreme Court affirms or reverses the decision of a lower court, or sends back (remands) the case for further proceedings

defendant—party against whom legal action is taken

deny—to turn down a petition or other request

determination—a decision by a court or administrative agency

dismiss the charges—to drop a complaint against an arrested person for lack of evidence

disqualify—to make ineligible, as when judges disqualify themselves from sitting in a case because of some possible interest in the outcome

dissenting opinion (dissent)—one disagreeing with the majority opinion of the Court

District Court, United States—a court in which federal civil and criminal cases, as well as suits between citizens of different states, are tried. Each state has one or more District Courts

docket—a list or calendar of cases to be decided in a specific term

doctrine—a principle of law used in deciding cases

due process of law—reasonable procedures according to the law of the land, including a fair trial with opportunity to face one's accusers and be heard in defense. Interfering with freedom of speech, press, or religion is held to deprive people of liberty without due process of law

elastic clause—the clause that stretches the power of Congress by giving it the right "to make all laws which shall be necessary and proper for carrying into execution the foregoing powers, and all other powers vested by this Constitution in the government of the United States, or in any department or officer thereof"

equity—a system of justice developed in English chancery courts to offer more flexible remedies than those available in common-law courts. An example of equity is an injunction ordering a person to stop doing something harmful, rather than waiting till the damage is done. Our federal courts and many higher state courts hear cases in both law and equity

ex post facto law—a law making a crime of an action done in the past, or increasing the punishment for it. Neither the federal government nor the states may pass ex post facto laws

federal question—one making it necessary to find out the meaning of a federal law, treaty, or constitutional provision in order to decide a case. Cases may go from state courts to the Supreme Court only when a federal question arises

First Amendment freedoms—freedom of religion, free speech, a free press, and freedom to meet and petition the government for a redress of grievances. Free discussion is so vital in a democracy that the Supreme Court has held that neither the federal government nor a state may restrict it except when it creates "a clear and present danger" of bringing about serious evils that the government has a right to prevent

friendly suit—a suit to test a law. The parties are not real adversaries and the Supreme Court will not hear such a case

general welfare clause—the opening clause of Article I, Section 8, of the Constitution, empowering Congress "to lay and collect taxes, duties, imposts and excises, to pay the debts and provide for common defense and general welfare of the United States." The Supreme Court has held that Congress may tax and spend for a purpose serving the general welfare, whether mentioned in the Constitution or not

government of limited powers—one limited by a written or unwritten constitution. Our federal government has limited powers over the states and the people

grand jury—see *jury*

habeas corpus—Latin for "you have the body." A writ of habeas corpus orders someone who is holding a person to bring the prisoner bodily into court. The judge decides whether the prisoner is being lawfully detained

indictment—an accusation by a grand jury, charging someone with a crime upon evidence presented by the public prosecutor

in forma pauperis—Latin for "in the manner of a poor person."

A method by which a poor person may bring a case to court without being liable for costs

injunction—a court order forbidding someone to harm another person's interests

jeopardy—peril, such as the danger of punishment faced by a defendant on trial. No person may be twice put in jeopardy for the same federal offense (Fifth Amendment)

judgment—a court's decision or sentence of law

judicial power—power of a court to decide cases and controversies under the laws

judicial review—the Court's examination of a law to find out whether it is in harmony with the Constitution or with federal laws and treaties. More broadly, "judicial review" means reconsidering a case decided in a lower court

jurisdiction—the extent of a court's authority. It may be limited by area or by specific types of cases, as determined by Congress

jury—a body of impartial citizens who examine evidence placed before them, looking for the truth. A grand jury hears complaints and makes accusations of crime. A trial jury, or petit jury, determines the guilt or innocence of an accused person

opinion—the Court's statement of the decision reached in a case, and an explanation of the law of the case and the reasoning by which this decision was reached

original jurisdiction—power to hear a case at its beginning. The Supreme Court has original jurisdiction when one of the parties is a state or a foreign diplomat (actually, the State Department handles most disputes involving diplomats). In other cases, the Court has appellate jurisdiction; it hears cases on appeal

overrule—to reject the authority of an earlier decision by deciding the same question of law the opposite way

petitioner—one who asks, or petitions, the Court to use its authority, as by issuing a writ of certiorari, to bring a case from a lower court for review

plaintiff—the party who begins an action; the complainant

police power—governmental power to protect the people's health, safety, and welfare

political question—one to be settled by the legislative or executive branches of government, not by the Court. Examples: How long do the states have to ratify a proposed amendment to the Constitution? Is a treaty with another nation still in effect?

precedent—a court decision that serves as an example in deciding similar cases

procedural rights—in federal cases, the protection of procedures set forth in the Bill of Rights and in federal laws; in state cases, the fundamentals of a fair trial by due process of law

quorum—six of the nine Justices are a quorum for hearing and deciding cases. If the vote is a tie, the decision of the lower court stands, but the Supreme Court will consider rehearing the case. A state or federal law is never invalidated unless five or more Justices so vote

recess—an interval of two weeks or longer between sittings, when opinions are prepared

remand—to send a case back to a lower court for further action

respondent—the party opposing the petitioner in a case

reverse—to overturn or set aside the judgment of a lower court

self-incrimination, privilege against—the right not to testify against oneself (Fifth Amendment)

separation of powers—division of governmental power among the legislative, executive, and judicial branches, so that one will check or balance another. James Madison, the "Father of the Constitution," said, "It may be a reflection

[55]

on human nature that such devices should be necessary to control the abuses of government. But what is government itself but the greatest of all reflections on human nature? If men were angels, no government would be necessary."

session—each day's sitting of the Court

sitting—a session; an open meeting of the Court where business is conducted

solicitor general—an officer of the Department of Justice (ranking next after the attorney general) who represents the interests of the United States in cases before the Supreme Court

statute—a law enacted by a legislature

stay—to hold up or halt the carrying out of a judicial sentence

supreme law of the land—the Constitution, laws made in pursuance thereof, and treaties made under the authority of the United States; based on the supremacy clause in Article VI of the Constitution

term—the time when the Court is sitting or in recess: from the first Monday in October till June or later. A special term is occasionally held in the summer to hear an urgent case of national importance

treaty-making power—the President's power to make treaties with the advice and consent of the Senate. Congress may pass necessary and proper laws for carrying out the terms of a treaty, as, for example, by protecting birds that migrate between the United States and Canada. Without a treaty, it couldn't; the birds are not in interstate commerce

trial—a court proceeding in which the facts of a case are examined

trial court—a court where cases are tried; not an appellate court, which reviews the law applied to cases already tried

unconstitutional—not in agreement with the Constitution, and hence of no effect

United States Reports—the published volumes of Supreme Court opinions, as prepared by the Reporter of Decisions

uphold—to find a law valid

war power—the combined powers of Congress and the President to wage war effectively. It is supported by several constitutional provisions, but would exist anyway, according to the Supreme Court, as part of the power over foreign affairs that passed to the United States upon declaring its independence. The war power, though vast, is not unlimited, the Court having held that "the Constitution of the United States is a law for rulers and people, equally in war and peace."

writ—a formal court order requiring a person to do, or to refrain from doing, some action

JUSTICES OF THE SUPREME COURT

(Chief Justices in Italics)

NAME	APPOINTED FROM	SERVED
John Jay	N.Y.	1789–1795
John Rutledge	S.C.	1789–1791
William Cushing	Mass.	1789–1810
James Wilson	Pa.	1789–1798
John Blair	Va.	1789–1796
James Iredell	N.C.	1790–1799
Thomas Johnson	Md.	1791–1793
William Paterson	N.J.	1793–1806
* *John Rutledge*	S.C.	1795–1795
Samuel Chase	Md.	1796–1811
Oliver Ellsworth	Conn.	1796–1800
Bushrod Washington	Va.	1798–1829
Alfred Moore	N.C.	1799–1804
John Marshall	Va.	1801–1835
William Johnson	S.C.	1804–1834
Brockholst Livingston	N.Y.	1806–1823
Thomas Todd	Ky.	1807–1826
Joseph Story	Mass.	1811–1845
Gabriel Duval	Md.	1811–1835
Smith Thompson	N.Y.	1823–1843
Robert Trimble	Ky.	1826–1828
John McLean	Ohio	1829–1861
Henry Baldwin	Pa.	1830–1844
James M. Wayne	Ga.	1835–1867
Roger B. Taney	Md.	1836–1864

| | APPOINTED | |
NAME	FROM	SERVED
Philip P. Barbour	Va.	1836–1841
John Catron	Tenn.	1837–1865
John McKinley	Ala.	1837–1852
Peter V. Daniel	Va.	1841–1860
Samuel Nelson	N.Y.	1845–1872
Levi Woodbury	N.H.	1845–1851
Robert C. Grier	Pa.	1846–1870
Benjamin R. Curtis	Mass.	1851–1857
John A. Campbell	Ala.	1853–1861
Nathan Clifford	Maine	1858–1881
Noah H. Swayne	Ohio	1862–1881
Samuel F. Miller	Iowa	1862–1890
David Davis	Ill.	1862–1877
Stephen J. Field	Calif.	1863–1897
Salmon P. Chase	Ohio	1864–1873
William Strong	Pa.	1870–1880
Joseph P. Bradley	N.J.	1870–1892
Ward Hunt	N.Y.	1873–1882
Morrison R. Waite	Ohio	1874–1888
John M. Harlan	Ky.	1877–1911
William B. Woods	Ga.	1881–1887
Stanley Matthews	Ohio	1881–1889
Horace Gray	Mass.	1882–1902
Samuel Blatchford	N.Y.	1882–1893
Lucius Q. C. Lamar	Miss.	1888–1893
Melville W. Fuller	Ill.	1888–1910
David J. Brewer	Kan.	1890–1910
Henry B. Brown	Mich.	1891–1906
George Shiras, Jr.	Pa.	1892–1903

NAME	APPOINTED FROM	SERVED
Howell E. Jackson	Tenn.	1893–1895
Edward D. White	La.	1894–1910
Rufus W. Peckham	N.Y.	1896–1909
Joseph McKenna	Calif.	1898–1925
Oliver Wendell Holmes	Mass.	1902–1932
William R. Day	Ohio	1903–1922
William H. Moody	Mass.	1906–1910
Horace H. Lurton	Tenn.	1910–1914
Edward D. White	La.	1910–1921
Charles Evans Hughes	N.Y.	1910–1916
Willis Van Devanter	Wyo.	1911–1937
Joseph R. Lamar	Ga.	1911–1916
Mahlon Pitney	N.J.	1912–1922
James C. McReynolds	Tenn.	1914–1941
Louis D. Brandeis	Mass.	1916–1939
John H. Clarke	Ohio	1916–1922
William Howard Taft	Conn.	1921–1930
George Sutherland	Utah	1922–1938
Pierce Butler	Minn.	1923–1939
Edward T. Sanford	Tenn.	1923–1930
Harlan F. Stone	N.Y.	1925–1941
Charles Evans Hughes	N.Y.	1930–1941
Owens J. Roberts	Pa.	1930–1945
Benjamin N. Cardozo	N.Y.	1932–1938
Hugo L. Black	Ala.	1937–1971
Stanley F. Reed	Ky.	1938–1957
Felix Frankfurter	Mass.	1939–1962
William O. Douglas	Conn.	1939–1975
Frank Murphy	Mich.	1940–1949

	APPOINTED	
NAME	FROM	SERVED
Harlan F. Stone	N.Y.	1941–1946
James F. Byrnes	S.C.	1941–1942
Robert H. Jackson	N.Y.	1941–1954
Wiley B. Rutledge	Iowa	1943–1949
Harold H. Burton	Ohio	1945–1958
Fred M. Vinson	Ky.	1946–1953
Tom C. Clark	Tex.	1949–1967
Sherman Minton	Ind.	1949–1956
Earl Warren	Calif.	1953–1969
John M. Harlan	N.Y.	1955–1971
William J. Brennan, Jr.	N.J.	1956–
Charles E. Whittaker	Mo.	1957–1962
Potter Stewart	Ohio	1958–
Byron R. White	Col.	1962–
Arthur J. Goldberg	Ill.	1962–1965
Abe Fortas	Tenn.	1965–1969
Thurgood Marshall	N.Y.	1967–
Warren E. Burger	Minn.	1969–
Harry A. Blackmun	Minn.	1970–
Lewis F. Powell, Jr.	Va.	1971–
William H. Rehnquist	Ariz.	1971–
John Paul Stevens	Ill.	1975–

° Recess appointment; presided over August term, but later rejected by Senate

FOR FURTHER READING

Congressional Research Service. *The Constitution of the United States of America, Analysis and Interpretation.* Washington, D.C.: U.S. Government Printing Office, 1973.

Congressional Quarterly, Inc. *Guide to the United States Supreme Court.* Washington, D.C.: Congressional Quarterly, Inc., 1977.

———. *The Supreme Court: Justice and the Law.* Washington, D.C.: Congressional Quarterly, Inc., 1977.

Forte, David F. *The Supreme Court.* New York: Franklin Watts, 1979.

Foundation of the Federal Bar Association. *Equal Justice Under Law: The Supreme Court in American Life.* New York: Grosset and Dunlop, 1975.

Ginger, Ann F. *The Law, the Supreme Court, and the People's Right.* Woodbury, New York: Barron's Educational Series, 1977.

McCloskey, Robert G. *The American Supreme Court.* Chicago: The University of Chicago Press, 1960.

Marquardt, Dorothy A. *A Guide to the Supreme Court.* Indianapolis/New York: The Bobbs-Merrill Company, 1977.

Salimon, Leon I., ed. *The Supreme Court.* New York: The H. W. Wilson Company, 1961.

Swisher, Carl Brent. *Historic Decisions of the Supreme Court.* New York: Van Nostrand Reinhold, 1969.

Warren, Charles. *The Supreme Court in United States History.* Boston: Little, Brown, and Company, 1926.

INDEX